BANKS

A Money Power Book

by DAVID A. ADLER

illustrated by
Tom Huffman

BANKS

WHERE THE MONEY IS

Franklin Watts

New York   London   Toronto   Sydney

1985

To Dad
A Great Teacher

R.L. 3.1 Spache Revised Formula

Library of Congress Cataloging in Publication Data

Adler, David A.
  Banks: where the money is.

  (A Money power book)
  Summary: Explains how a bank works through its
functions of saving, lending, the use of checks, and
other aspects of banking.
  1. Banks and banking—Juvenile literature. [1. Banks
and banking] I. Huffman, Tom, ill. II. Title. III. Series.
HG1609.A35 1985   332.1   85-8848
ISBN 0-531-04878-0

Library of Congress Cataloging in Publication Data

Text copyright © 1985 by David A. Adler
Illustrations copyright © 1985 by Franklin Watts, Inc.
All rights reserved
Printed in the United States of America
6 5 4 3 2 1

Have you ever owned a piggy bank?

It's easy to understand how a piggy bank works. A piggy bank is a good place to save coins. You drop coins in. And when you need the money, you open the piggy bank and take the money out.

But what if you have a lot of money, hundreds of dollars? A piggy bank isn't the best place to keep large sums of money. It might be stolen. The best place to keep money safe is in a large bank with guards and insurance to protect your money. It should be a bank that puts your money to work.

What is a bank? How does it work?

The business of banking is thousands of years old. In ancient Babylonia, almost four thousand years ago, **promises** were written on wet clay. These were promises one person made to pay a certain weight of silver or copper to someone else. These promises were like the **checks** people write today. After the promise was written, the clay was baked. It became as hard as stone. Some of these "first checks" are still around, in museums.

Banking as we know it today began about four hundred years ago in Italy. The Bank of Venice borrowed money from the people of Venice. The bank paid a fee to the people and then loaned the money to the government. This fee was called **interest.** The country was at war and the government used the money to pay the army.

The word **bank** comes from the Italian word "banca," which means "bench." The early Italian bankers did their banking on benches set up in the street.

Banking began in the United States in 1781. That's when the Bank of North America was founded in Philadelphia. It was the country's first successful bank. It printed **bank notes**—money. And it loaned money to people starting businesses. Alexander Hamilton, the first Secretary of the Treasury, believed that banks were needed to lend money to new industries to help them grow.

During the country's early years, banks issued their own money. Each bank note they issued was a printed promise. It was a promise that the note could be exchanged at the bank for silver or gold.

In the mid-1800s there were thousands of different bank notes. But many of the banks did not have enough silver or gold. The promise that all their money could be exchanged for silver or gold was a lie.

Then in the 1860s the government passed laws stopping banks from printing money. There would be a national **currency.** All the money would be printed by the United States government.

Banks don't print money anymore, but they do *create* money. How do they do this?

People deposit money in banks. If they open a **checking account,** the bank gives them blank checks. Each of those checks must be filled in with the amount to be paid and the signature of the owner of the account. Then it's as good as money. It can be used to pay for things.

When your mother writes a check to the telephone company, she is not really creating money. The check is an order to the bank to give the telephone company some of the money she already has deposited in her account. Your mother isn't *creating* money. She's just transferring it from one account to another, from her account to the telephone company's account.

But the bank does create money. If your
mother opens a checking account with a deposit of
$1,000, she can write one or more checks that
together total $1,000. If none of the money is used,
the blank checks in her pocket are worth up to
$1,000.

Your mother has $1,000, and so does the
bank. But the bank doesn't simply hold onto the
money and wait for your mother to spend it. They
try to lend it to someone.

If someone borrows $500 from the bank to buy a used car, and the money comes from your mother's account, the bank has created an extra $500.

How?

Your mother began with $1,000 in bills and coins, which she deposited in her checking account. Your mother still has her blank checks. She can still write checks for up to the $1,000 she has deposited in her account. And, there's someone with $500, which will be spent on a car. Now there is $1,500 that can be used to buy things. In effect, there are now 500 extra dollars. The bank has created money.

Why do people need checks?

A check is easier to use than coins or paper bills. A check can be written for any amount and sent through the mail. It's much easier and safer to send a check each month through the mail to pay the telephone bill than it would be to bring the exact amount of money owed to the telephone company office.

Checks are easier and safer to carry than coins and paper bills. Most people wouldn't be comfortable carrying thousands of dollars in coins and bills. All those coins and bills might be heavy. And they might be lost or stolen.

But people can easily carry a check that can be filled in and become worth thousands of dollars. If a blank check is lost or stolen, the owner hasn't lost money. A blank check is worthless. It can only be used as money when it is filled in and signed by the owner of the account. And, if the check is written to a certain person or company, only that person or company can exchange the check for cash.

Most of the money paid from one person to another, from one company to another, is paid by check.

What happens to the checks people write?

Checks for many thousands of dollars may be deposited in a bank each day, checks written by **depositors** of other banks. The bank will want to collect that money.

And a bank's depositors may write checks worth thousands of dollars to people with accounts in other banks. The bank will have to transfer that money to the other banks.

Banks send the checks they have collected to local **clearinghouses,** places which add up how much each bank owes the others in the area. Checks from banks outside the area are sent to central clearinghouses.

Why must banks lend out depositors' money?

A bank is a business. Banks make their profit by lending money. When they lend money, they charge **interest.**

Interest is the fee banks charge for the money they lend. If the yearly rate of interest is 15 percent, then if someone borrowed $100 for one year, at the end of the year he or she would owe $115. At the end of two years he or she would owe $130. The more people borrow and the longer they hold the money, the more interest they'll owe.

But if people have to pay interest, why do they borrow money?

They need the money. A young couple buying a house may not have all the money they need, so they will borrow from a bank. Someone might borrow to buy a new car or to buy new machinery for a factory. They can use the car and the machinery *while* they repay the loan.

Banks need your money and the money of other depositors. Depositors are the people who have savings accounts, checking accounts, and holiday gift accounts. They are all the people who keep their money in a bank.

Banks need depositors' money to lend to other people to buy homes, cars, and machinery. Banks advertise for new depositors. They even offer gifts. And they pay interest.

Of course, a bank pays a lower interest rate to its depositors than it charges on its loans. That's how a bank makes a profit.

But how can the bank lend your mother's money? What if your mother wants to spend it all?

Your mother is not the only depositor in the bank. She is one of a great many people who keep what together is a huge sum of money in the bank. The bank knows that not every one of their depositors will want his or her money at the same time. And they know that as some people take money out of the bank, others will be putting money in.

But still, the bank doesn't lend all of the money deposited. They keep money in reserve for depositors who may wish to withdraw money. The more money deposited in a bank, the more the bank must keep in reserve. The bank must be prepared in case people suddenly want to withdraw large sums of money.

Is money *really* safe in a bank?

Banks have guards, vaults, and insurance.
Most banks in the United States are members of
the Federal Deposit Insurance Corporation (FDIC).
Each account is insured for up to $100,000. If a
member bank cannot pay depositors wishing to
withdraw money, the FDIC will pay them. The FDIC
will also lend money to member banks in need
of help.

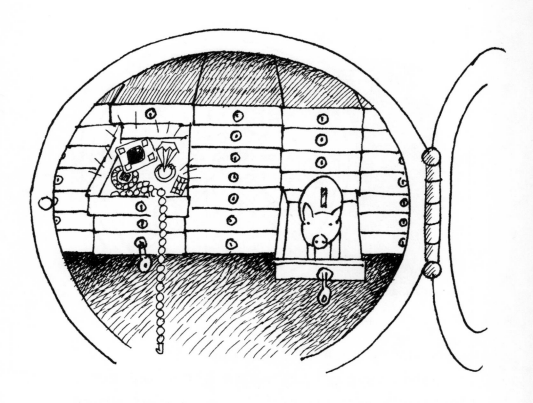

Banks keep depositors' money safe and they lend money. Do they do anything else?

Banks have safe-deposit boxes that they rent. These metal boxes are fireproof and are locked in huge vaults. They're a safe place to keep jewelry, important papers, and other valuables.

Some banks help people manage their money, with special accounts for retirement. They also manage **trust** accounts, money put aside by one person for someone else.

Banks help people pay their bills with different forms of checks.

Certified checks are checks that the bank guarantees are good. They guarantee that there is enough money available in the account to pay for the check when it is cashed.

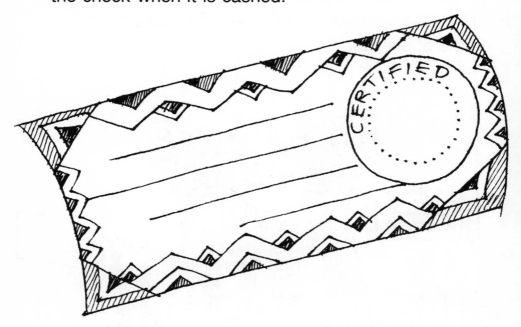

People without checking accounts might buy cashiers' checks, registered checks, or money orders. Once someone buys one of these, the bank sets money aside and is responsible to pay for the check when it's cashed.

Some banks also issue credit cards. With these
cards, people buy things, sign a form, and pay
sometime later for what they bought.

Banking is no longer done on street benches. Banks today lend people the money they need to buy houses and cars and to start businesses. Banks lend people in business the money they need to buy machinery and to build new factories. Banks keep depositors' money safe, and when banks lend out that money, they help our country grow.